Original title:
Shimmering Skies

Copyright © 2024 Swan Charm
All rights reserved.

Author: Liina Liblikas
ISBN HARDBACK: 978-9916-79-957-4
ISBN PAPERBACK: 978-9916-79-958-1
ISBN EBOOK: 978-9916-79-959-8

Harmonics of the Sky

In twilight's glow, the stars appear,
They whisper secrets, soft and clear.
The moonlight dances on the sea,
A symphony of whispers free.

Clouds drift softly, like a sigh,
Painting dreams across the sky.
Each star a note, a gentle tune,
A lullaby for night's cocoon.

The breeze carries a tender hum,
Nature's chorus, calm and drum.
With every breath, the night expands,
An echo felt in distant lands.

Colors blend as dawn draws near,
Awakening the world from fear.
The sun will rise, a vibrant spark,
Illuminating shadows dark.

In harmony, the heavens sing,
A tribute to the life they bring.
From deep below to heights above,
The sky reflects our quest for love.

Canvas of Celestial Bliss

Underneath the starry skies,
Dreams are painted, soft and wise.
Each twinkle speaks of distant lands,
Where hope and wonder gently stand.

Colors blend in twilight's glow,
Mysteries in the night can flow.
The canvas stretches, ever wide,
A journey forged beneath the tide.

Chasing the Distant Gleam

In the horizon, shadows play,
Chasing dreams that fade away.
With every step, a story grows,
The heart, a compass, knows where to go.

Through valleys deep and mountains high,
We seek the gleam that draws the eye.
Each moment passed, a fleeting sight,
Fueling the fire, igniting the night.

Rays of Whispering Light

Softly beneath the morning sun,
Whispers travel, old yet fun.
Each ray a promise, warm and bright,
Filling the world with pure delight.

In golden hues, the day awakes,
Casting shadows, calm and breaks.
The dance of light, a gentle sigh,
Awakens dreams that softly lie.

The Brushstrokes of Evening

As day retreats in shades of blue,
Brushstrokes blend, creating hue.
The sun dips low, a fiery kiss,
Wrapping the world in evening bliss.

Stars emerge in velvet skies,
Each one born from whispered sighs.
In quiet wonder, night descends,
The brush of darkness, where magic bends.

Echoes of Radiance in the Veil

In whispers soft, the shadows play,
As twilight drapes the end of day.
Each star ignites in velvet night,
Echoes of dreams in silver light.

A distant song, a haunting call,
Its gentle touch, it weaves through all.
The veil of time, so thin, so near,
Reflects our hopes, both bold and clear.

The moonlit path begins to shine,
An ancient dance, forever thine.
With every step, the heart will sway,
Where echoes linger, love will stay.

The Golden Hour's Embrace

As day dissolves in hues of gold,
The canvas brightens, secrets told.
Each shadow stretches, yawns with grace,
In the golden hour's warm embrace.

Light kisses earth, a gentle stroke,
Fleeting moments, softly woke.
Nature whispers, peace unfolds,
In hues of amber, life beholds.

The world ignites in radiant glee,
As dusk dances by the cascading sea.
The horizon glows, a lover's sigh,
In this embrace, we rise and fly.

Breathing Light into Dusk

The sun dips low, a quiet sigh,
As day prepares to say goodbye.
In twilight's hush, dreams let us soar,
Breathing light as shadows pour.

Each flicker bold, a star is born,
In dusky shades, the night is worn.
We wander paths of whispered thought,
Where echoes linger, time is caught.

With every breath, the world aligns,
In twilight's grace, our spirit shines.
We find our peace as darkness calls,
Breathing light until night falls.

Where Dreams Touch the Heavens

In a realm where wishes weave,
Where hearts find courage to believe.
The stars align in jeweled skies,
Where dreams ascend and spirits rise.

With every hope, a feathered flight,
We chase the dawn, embrace the light.
The universe hums a poetic song,
As we dance where we belong.

Beneath the moon's enchanting gaze,
We craft our futures, set ablaze.
In this expanse, we intertwine,
Where dreams touch heavens, pure and divine.

The Celestial Dialogue

In the night sky, stars converse,
Whispers of dreams in the universe.
Galaxies twirl in silent flight,
Echoes of wisdom, cloaked in light.

Comets streak with tales untold,
Carrying secrets, both new and old.
The moon listens with a silver glow,
Guiding the tides and the winds that blow.

Constellations, dressed in time,
Sketching stories in the sublime.
Each twinkle holds a wish or fear,
A cosmic bond, forever near.

Planets hum a gentle tune,
Dancing softly beneath the moon.
In the vast expanse, hearts align,
A celestial bond, pure and divine.

Beneath this canvas, souls find peace,
In harmony, their worries cease.
A dialogue of hopes and dreams,
In the night sky, life redeems.

Light's Gentle Cascade

Morning breaks with a soft embrace,
Golden rays in a tender chase.
Whispers of warmth kiss the air,
Filling the world with vibrant flair.

Sunbeams stream through leafy greens,
Painting the earth with whispered scenes.
Nature awakens, ready to bloom,
As light dispels the lingering gloom.

Shadows retreat from the dawn's grace,
Illuminating every hidden space.
In this glow, hearts start to sing,
Celebrating the joy that light can bring.

Rivers of sunlight gently flow,
Leading us where wildflowers grow.
A cascade of colors, vivid and bright,
Transforming the world in morning light.

As dusk falls, colors intertwine,
A sacred dance, both yours and mine.
In every moment, a chance to find,
The beauty and light that love entwined.

A Horizon of Endless Possibilities

Beyond the hills, the sun will rise,
Painting the sky with hopes that fly.
Each dawn a canvas, vast and bright,
Showing dreams in vibrant light.

Paths stretch wide, in every direction,
Choices await in sweet reflection.
Each step forward, a brand new chance,
A horizon where dreams can dance.

Waves of courage crash on the shore,
Calling the brave to explore once more.
Beyond the limits we've known so far,
A future shines, a guiding star.

In the whispers of wind, hear the call,
Adventure awaits, promising all.
With every heartbeat, a wish unfurls,
In open skies, the journey swirls.

A world awaits, with arms open wide,
Embracing spirits that dare to glide.
In the twilight of endless skies,
Possibilities rise, and hope complies.

The Dance of Light and Shadow

In twilight's glow, shadows waltz,
Merging softly, they find their faults.
Chasing light through the trees that sway,
A rhythmic pulse in night and day.

Flashes of brilliance spark the dark,
Guiding paths, igniting a spark.
In every contrast, life reveals,
The depth of joy, the ache it yields.

Silhouettes twirl in a gentle breeze,
Weaving stories beneath the trees.
Light plays tricks on the muted ground,
Where beauty in darkness may be found.

Each flicker a moment, distinct and bold,
The warmth of light in the night's hold.
In the dance of contrasts, we see,
The balance of life's mystery.

As day fades and night takes her throne,
Light and shadow find their own.
Together they flow, an ageless song,
In this dance, we all belong.

The Secret Language of Stars

In the night sky, whispers glide,
Stories of old in silence bide.
Each twinkle a word, soft and bright,
A cosmic tale in the blanket of night.

Constellations speak in a dance,
Guiding dreams with a fleeting glance.
The moon, a listener, silently sighs,
As wishes are cast under velvet skies.

Galaxies swirl in a timeless trance,
Infinite truths in a heavenly dance.
Stars weave their secrets, a radiant thread,
A universal verse that must be read.

Faint echoes of laughter, light years away,
Stardust memories in twilight's play.
Awakening hope with each rising glow,
A celestial language only hearts know.

Celestial Dances on the Breeze

Whispers of twilight on gentle wings,
Celestial dancers, the nightingale sings.
Moonlight twirls with shadows in flight,
Painting the heavens, soft and bright.

Stars pirouette in the deep, dark sea,
Guided by winds, forever free.
A symphony hums in the cool of the night,
As constellations flicker, a wondrous sight.

Galaxies waltz, their steps so divine,
Beneath the celestial curtain, they intertwine.
Each fold of the wind carries a song,
Echoing softly, where we belong.

In the shimmer of starlight, dreams take flight,
Spirits of evening, pure delight.
Echoes embrace in the dance of the breeze,
Holding the night in a tranquil tease.

Vesper's Glimmering Horizon

At dusk's soft arrival, the world takes a breath,
Colors of twilight weave beauty in depth.
Violet hues kiss the edge of the day,
As stars quietly gather, lighting the way.

On the horizon, secrets awake,
Whispers of night, a gentle shake.
The sun bids farewell, a fiery embrace,
While shadows rise up in a delicate race.

Clouds drift like dreams, in a canvas of gold,
Rays of connection, a story retold.
Vesper's chorus hums, a soft serenade,
Painting our thoughts in the evening shade.

Every heartbeat echoes the call of the night,
Wrapped in the magic, so lush, so bright.
Glimmers of hope, in the twilight's sheen,
We find solace where beauty has been.

Threads of Dusk in the Sky

Threads of dusk weave through the air,
A tapestry rich, beyond compare.
Hues blend and mingle, a painter's delight,
Embers of day fold gently to night.

In the silence, the stars softly gleam,
Losers and winners in twilight's dream.
A dance of shadows, a tender embrace,
Transition of worlds, a sacred space.

Time drifts on as day meets the night,
In the cradle of darkness, all feels right.
Breathing in magic, the horizon anew,
Revealing the wonders that softly ensue.

Threads of hope wrap around the sky,
Whispers of dreams that never die.
Each lingering moment, a promise to keep,
In the arms of dusk, where secrets seep.

The Dance of Celestial Bodies

In the night, the stars align,
Spinning tales in silver shine.
Planets twirl in cosmic grace,
A ballet in the darkened space.

Comets streak with fiery tails,
Whispering of forgotten trails.
Galaxies in distant flight,
A dance that fills the velvet night.

Moonlight glows on tranquil seas,
Caressing dreams on gentle breeze.
Sunrise paints the world anew,
With colors vibrant, warm, and true.

Each orbit tells a timeless tale,
Celestial rhythms never fail.
Harmony in vast expanse,
The universe in a cosmic dance.

Eons pass with radiant light,
As stars continue their silent flight.
In this dance, we find our place,
Among the bodies, full of grace.

Ethereal Reflections

Whispers of the moonlit night,
Dance upon the waves of light.
Mirrored visions softly gleam,
Crafting pathways of a dream.

In the stillness, shadows play,
Painting stories in the gray.
Ethers drift, a gentle sigh,
Echoes of the worlds nearby.

Stars above, like lanterns bright,
Guide our souls through endless flight.
In their glow, we find our muse,
Wonders that we cannot lose.

Clouds reflect the sun's embrace,
Softly weaving through the space.
Nature sings, a tranquil song,
In reflections, we belong.

At dawn's break, the colors bloom,
Ethereal light dispels the gloom.
In these moments, we can see,
The magic of eternity.

Skyward Hopes

Gazing up to endless skies,
Where dreams take flight and hope will rise.
Clouds like cotton, soft and bright,
Whisper secrets of the night.

From the earth, our spirits yearn,
For the stars, a bright return.
Winds of change, they lift our hearts,
As the dawn of hope departs.

Every star a dream we chase,
Reflections of our inner grace.
Beneath the vast and endless dome,
Skyward hopes lead us back home.

With each breath, we reach afar,
Guided by our wish on a star.
In that glow, our futures spark,
Illuminating paths through dark.

In the night, we write our fate,
In the heavens, we elate.
Let our hearts not be confined,
For in the sky, our hopes align.

The Echoes of Dusk

As twilight falls with gentle grace,
The world is wrapped in a soft embrace.
Colors blend, the day must rest,
In hushed whispers, nature's best.

Crickets sing in evening's glow,
As shadows stretch, the breezes flow.
Stars awaken, one by one,
To cradle dreams until the sun.

The horizon wears a golden crown,
While whispers of the night come down.
With each sigh, the past returns,
In echoes where our memory burns.

Moonlit pathways softly gleam,
Leading us to realms of dream.
In the quiet, hearts will find,
The echoes linger, intertwined.

As dusk unfolds its velvet hands,
We gather hopes like grains of sands.
In every echo, love persists,
In the twilight, our souls coexist.

Prism of the Night

Stars twinkle in the dark,
Whispers of the dreams they spark.
Moonlight dances on the sea,
Secrets held in mystery.

Shadows waltz beneath the trees,
Night's embrace is soft as fleece.
Gentle breezes tell their tales,
Carried forth on soothing gales.

Colors swirl in twilight's hue,
Painting night in shades so true.
Silver glimmers on the ground,
In this peace, our hearts are found.

The world draped in a velvet shroud,
Silent dreams begin to crowd.
In the stillness, hope ignites,
Holding tight to starry nights.

With each breath, the night unfolds,
Glories whispered, love retold.
In the prism of the night,
Endless wonders, pure delight.

The Language of Light

Sunrise spills its golden beams,
Awakening our brightest dreams.
Colors dance upon the dawn,
Nature's canvas stretched and drawn.

Morning whispers soft and clear,
Bringing all that we hold dear.
Light unveils the world's embrace,
Each shadow finds its rightful place.

In gentle shades of pink and red,
A tranquil palette overhead.
Every hue a tale to share,
Filling hearts with warmth and care.

Midday sun begins to glow,
Painting paths where we will go.
In its rays, our spirits soar,
Filling us with hope and more.

As day fades to twilight's grace,
Light reveals a sacred space.
In its glow, we find our might,
Speaking softly, the language of light.

Hues of Infinity

Beyond the stars, the colors blend,
Timeless patterns that transcend.
Endless shades of cosmic light,
Whispering secrets of the night.

Every hue a story spun,
Infinity has just begun.
Vibrations in the void so deep,
Echoes stirring from their sleep.

Galaxies in vivid dance,
Daring all to take a chance.
In the dark, potentials bloom,
Painting vastness as we loom.

Rivers of color intertwine,
In every shade, a spark divine.
We are bits of light and sound,
Connected in the world around.

In this masterpiece, we find
The colors speak, the heart aligned.
Hues of infinity take flight,
Cascading down through endless night.

Painted Dreams Above

Clouds like brushes, soft and light,
Sketch the visions, day and night.
Each stroke tells a tale untold,
Woven dreams in strands of gold.

Sunset's palette spreads and glows,
Blending reds with blues that flow.
Nature's art, a wondrous view,
Awakening the soul anew.

Stars emerge in velvet skies,
Whispers curious, tantalize.
Guided by the moon's soft grace,
We drift to a transcendent space.

In painted dreams, we lose all time,
Floating softly, heart in rhyme.
Each twinkle sparks a wish, a flight,
As we wander through the night.

In this gallery above, we roam,
Finding beauty far from home.
In painted dreams, our spirits soar,
Eternal wonders to explore.

Vivid Tapestries in the Air

Colors swirl in endless dance,
Threads of light in a fleeting trance.
Whispers weave through skies so bright,
A canvas born from day to night.

Birds take flight on painted wings,
Nature sings as the daylight springs.
Brushstrokes bold, horizons wide,
A masterpiece that won't abide.

Clouds like dreams drift and sway,
Tales of wonder in shades of gray.
Every hue a story told,
In vibrant threads, the world unfolds.

Fleeting moments, a painter's grace,
Captured souls in this vast space.
The heavens pulse, alive with fire,
In vivid tapestries, we aspire.

Beneath this art, we all reside,
In awe of skies, open wide.
Each breath a part of this grand affair,
Lives stitched together, vivid and rare.

The Luminous Embrace of Morning

Dawn spills light, a soft caress,
Kissing dreams as they coalesce.
Whispers of birds flutter near,
Morning's embrace, so warm and clear.

Golden rays break through the mist,
Nature stirs, none to resist.
Colors bloom in tranquil grace,
A symphony of time and space.

Gentle breezes play and tease,
Rustling leaves in tranquil ease.
The world awakens, fresh and bright,
In luminous warmth, day takes flight.

Every petal glistens, anew,
Kissed by dew, a dance in view.
Promises hang in the crisp air,
Morning's glow, a sacred prayer.

As the sun climbs high and bold,
Stories of beauty, gently unfold.
In each moment, a spark of glee,
A luminous embrace, wild and free.

Secrets Written in the Clouds

High above, the secrets lay,
In fluffy whispers, they softly play.
Shapes and shadows tell a tale,
In the azure, they gently sail.

Mysterious figures drift and weave,
Wonders hidden for us to conceive.
Each cloud a letter, a silent word,
In the sky's book, their stories heard.

Storms gather, tales of might,
Cumulus dreams, a stormy flight.
In every thunderous, roaring sound,
Lies a secret, profound and round.

The sun dips low, colors ignite,
Clouds blush boldly in fading light.
Every sunset, a promise bestowed,
The secrets of ages, softly bestowed.

Like whispers of the passing breeze,
Clouds hold tales that always please.
Look up and marvel, take a pause,
In secrets written, nature's laws.

Aurora's Kiss on the Land

Dancing lights in the velvet sky,
A ribbon of colors, a gentle sigh.
Stars watch closely from high above,
As nature envelops us in love.

Painting night with emerald glow,
Whispers of magic in the breeze flow.
Every flicker tells a tale,
In secret harmony, they unveil.

Cold winds carry warmth unseen,
An aurora's kiss, delicate and keen.
Soft waves of light, a fleeting show,
Wrapped in wonder, we breathe and glow.

Across the valleys, mountains grand,
Auroras paint with a gentle hand.
In silence, night breathes deep and slow,
While dreams intertwine in the gentle flow.

Let us gaze at this celestial spree,
With hearts lifted, wild and free.
Aurora's kiss lingers on our face,
A celestial dance, a divine embrace.

The Light Between Worlds

In twilight's calm, the shadows blend,
A whisper soft, where paths extend.
Between the realms, a glowing thread,
Guides weary souls, where hopes are fed.

With every step, a heartbeat's grace,
Illuminates the hidden space.
In the stillness, dreams take flight,
Cradled gently by the light.

A dance of stars, a glimmering sign,
In silence found, the stars align.
Across the bridge, we find our way,
To realms where night replaces day.

So take my hand, let's wander far,
Beneath the glow of each bright star.
Together bound, we'll redefine,
This sacred path, yours and mine.

In the light where worlds converge,
Our spirits soar, they surge and merge.
Between the beats of time and space,
We find the truth in love's embrace.

Aetherial Paintbrush

With strokes of dreams, the cosmos twirls,
A brush of light that paints the world.
Each color drips from starlit skies,
Creating realms where magic lies.

The canvas glows with hues unseen,
A symphony of the in-between.
Where thoughts can bloom like flowers bright,
In daydreams spun from darkest night.

A swirl of fate, the galaxies spin,
As whispers soft invite us in.
The aether hums with secrets old,
Unveiling stories yet untold.

Each stroke, a tale that longs to breathe,
Of love and loss, of joy and grief.
In every hue, a spark ignites,
A world reborn in endless nights.

So let us paint with fervent hearts,
The aether speaks, and art imparts.
In every shade, a journey start,
The universe, an endless art.

Dawn's First Embrace

When night gives way to tender light,
A whisper hushes, soft and bright.
The sky, adorned with blush and gold,
Awakens dreams that long were cold.

The dew-kissed earth begins to stir,
As daybreak dawns, our hearts confer.
With every ray, new hopes arise,
In dawn's embrace, the spirit flies.

Birds serenade the silent morn,
With melodies of joy reborn.
As shadows flee, the world unfolds,
A tapestry of warmth and gold.

The horizon glows, a promise made,
In every heartbeat, fears allayed.
The sun ascends with graceful ease,
In dawn's sweet light, our souls find peace.

So let us cherish each new day,
As dawn arrives to gently sway.
Together bound, in love's sweet grace,
We find our hope in dawn's embrace.

Cosmic Reflections

In starlit pools, the heavens stir,
Mirrors of time, where dreams confer.
Each sparkle held in cosmic sway,
Reflects the night, then fades away.

With every glance, a truth revealed,
A fleeting thought, our hearts unsealed.
In silence deep, the cosmos sighs,
As galaxies weave their lullabies.

The universe hums a tune divine,
In echoes soft, the stars align.
And in this dance of light and shade,
Our souls embrace the paths we've laid.

So let us dream beneath the skies,
As constellations mesmerize.
In cosmic truths, we find our place,
Reflections deep in time and space.

With every star, a wish unfolds,
As night unveils its secrets bold.
In cosmic depth, our spirits soar,
Together now, forevermore.

Ethereal Glow

In twilight's soft embrace we find,
A gentle light that warms the mind.
Flickers spark in the deepening night,
Whispers of dreams take their flight.

Glimmers dance on the silvered streams,
Painting the world in tranquil dreams.
A hush settles upon the land,
As magic weaves through every hand.

The horizon blushes, deep and wide,
Calling forth the stars to guide.
In every heart, a secret stays,
Illuminated by twilight's gaze.

Soft petals fall from the evening flower,
Nurtured by the moon's sweet power.
Awakening souls in the silent night,
Dancing beneath the soft starlight.

Each breath taken, a sacred vow,
Entranced by the wonders here and now.
In this realm where magic roams,
We find in shadows, joy that glows.

Celestial Dance

Stars collide in a whirl of grace,
The universe speaks in endless space.
Galaxies twirl with a radiant glow,
In this vast waltz, hearts will flow.

Moonlit beams spill on the sea,
Where night embraces all that's free.
Whirls of wind chase the fleeting sand,
As time stands still, like a gentle hand.

Comets race across the sky,
Drawing wishes that flutter and sigh.
Constellations paint tales of old,
In every shimmer, a story told.

A dance of shadows, light and dark,
In this rhythm, find your spark.
With every twirl in the midnight air,
Feel the magic, it's everywhere.

The cosmos breathes, a sweet embrace,
Guiding lost souls to their place.
In every heartbeat, a pulse of chance,
Join the wonder in celestial dance.

Glistening Horizons

At dawn's first light, a canvas wide,
Veils of mist where secrets hide.
Golden rays kiss the waking land,
As dreams stretch out, unfurling, grand.

Mountains rise with majestic pride,
Beneath the skies where hopes abide.
Waves of light break upon the shore,
Each glimmer whispers, 'Seek for more.'

Colors burst in a vibrant swirl,
As nature dances, hearts unfurl.
The air is sweet with the promise of day,
Inviting feet to wander and play.

Morning's breath, a gentle sigh,
Lifts the spirits, urging high.
With every step on this golden ground,
In glistening horizons, joy is found.

As sunlight spills in a joyous arc,
The world awakens, igniting the spark.
Each moment shines with a golden chance,
In this tapestry where our souls dance.

Veil of Stars

Beneath the cloak of endless night,
A tapestry woven with threads of light.
Stars whisper secrets, softly shared,
In this quiet, souls are bared.

The moon hangs high, a watchful eye,
Guiding dreams as we drift and sigh.
With every twinkle, a lullaby sung,
In this realm, we all belong.

Nebulae drift in colors bold,
Tales of night skies waiting to be told.
In the silence, echoes ring,
From the beauty that the cosmos brings.

Each constellation, a map divine,
Charting hopes, like bottles of wine.
In starlit paths, we lose our fears,
Finding our way through the dust of years.

As dawn approaches, the stars will fade,
Yet in our hearts, their glow won't jade.
For beneath this vast and shimmering dome,
In every star, there's a sense of home.

Radiance Above the Horizon

Golden beams break through the night,
Whispers of dawn take to flight.
Sky ablaze in hues of gold,
A new day's promise begins to unfold.

Clouds blush in the morning glow,
Hope arises, a gentle flow.
Birds chirp their sweet serenade,
As nature's beauty is displayed.

Mountains echo the sun's warm glow,
Shadows fade, and the world will know.
Every heart feels the soft light,
Radiance rising, banishing night.

Fields bloom in colors so bright,
Life awakens in pure delight.
Under the sky's radiant dome,
Each sunrise beckons us home.

In the stillness, dreams take flight,
Carried forth on beams of light.
Beneath the vast, eternal blue,
Radiance whispers, "Start anew."

Dusk's Embrace

As sunlight fades, shadows play,
A gentle hush marks the end of day.
Stars twinkle in the deepening sky,
Dusk's embrace, a soft goodbye.

Whispers of twilight fill the air,
Moments linger, tender and rare.
Colors blend in the fading light,
Embracing the magic of the night.

Crickets sing their evening tune,
The world bathed in silvered moon.
Clouds drift slowly, a soft parade,
In dusky hues, dreams are made.

Each branch sways in a soft caress,
Wrapping the earth in quietness.
With every shade, the day takes flight,
In the arms of calming night.

Time stands still in the twilight glow,
As shadows dance, both fast and slow.
Embrace the night, let worries cease,
In dusk's embrace, find your peace.

Twilight's Canvas

Brushstrokes of purple grace the sky,
As day gives way, the stars reply.
An artist's hand, soft and bold,
Painting tales in colors untold.

Cascading hues from blue to brown,
Twilight cloaks the sleepy town.
Whispers of dusk with secrets to share,
In the chill of evening, feel the air.

Rippling rivers reflect the light,
As shadows gather in delight.
Nature's palette, rich and vast,
Each moment precious, designed to last.

In this softness, dreams take wing,
Embracing the night, the calm it brings.
With every breath, we softly blend,
In twilight's canvas, hearts transcend.

Under the sky's ethereal brush,
Feel the world around you hush.
In every hue, let your spirit soar,
Twilight invites us to explore.

Luminous Dreams

In the stillness of the night,
Whispers turn to gentle light.
Dreams awaken, vivid and bright,
Guiding souls through endless flight.

Stars twinkle like thoughts set free,
Shimmering hopes in harmony.
Floating through a wondrous space,
Each dream a path, each heart a trace.

Moonlit visions softly call,
Embracing the depths of all.
Awakening thoughts that gently gleam,
In the night, we chase our dream.

Every heartbeat finds its rhyme,
A dance of spirit, a timeless climb.
In the ether, where wishes gleam,
The world transforms in luminous dream.

So close your eyes and drift away,
Through realms where dreams swim and sway.
In the glow of the night's embrace,
Find your truth in this sacred space.

Ribbons of Light

Soft whispers in the night,
Dancing through the sky,
Woven threads of silver bright,
As dreams began to fly.

Each glow a wish from hearts,
That travel far and wide,
In the dark, a canvas starts,
With love as our guide.

Coloring the air we breathe,
With hope and gentle care,
Illumination we believe,
As magic fills the air.

They twirl and spin, a sight,
Enchanting every soul,
In this dance of pure delight,
Where stories unfold whole.

The night whispers soft and sweet,
As the ribbons unite,
In a rhythm, hearts will beat,
Guided by the light.

Beneath the Starlit Veil

Shimmers in the midnight glow,
Whispers of the past,
Underneath the cosmic show,
Where shadows are cast.

The moon hangs like a dream,
In a cloak of deep blue,
Reflections softly beam,
A serenade so true.

Waves of silence ebb and flow,
In this tranquil place,
Beneath the stars' warm glow,
Embraced in their grace.

As secrets dance on high,
In the night's tender hold,
We gaze up to the sky,
With stories left untold.

Every flicker brings a smile,
A promise to keep near,
Beneath the starlit pile,
Our dreams will persevere.

Aurora's Serenade

Colors brush the morning sky,
As whispers coalesce,
A symphony of soft goodbye,
To nighttime's quiet press.

In hues of pink and gold,
The world begins to wake,
A tale of light is told,
In every breath we take.

Dancing lights begin to play,
Across the frosty morn,
In this sweet, enchanted ballet,
New hopes and dreams are born.

The echoes of the night,
Now fleeting like the breeze,
A canvas bathed in light,
Brings warmth with gentle ease.

With every rising sun,
A serenade will start,
In colors that will run,
A melody of heart.

Starlight Melodies

In the hush of twilight's grace,
Secrets softly hum,
Melodies that gently trace,
Where starlit dreams succumb.

Every twinkle holds a song,
Of wishes cast at night,
A symphony prolonged,
As hearts take flight.

Guided by the light above,
Each note begins to soar,
In the melody of love,
We find what we adore.

The night air, sweet and clear,
Recalls what long has passed,
Starlight always draws us near,
A harmony steadfast.

With every breeze a sound,
That calls us to believe,
In starlight, we are found,
In dreams, we shall achieve.

Transcendent Light Beyond the Clouds

In whispers soft, the dawn appears,
A golden hue that calms our fears.
Illuminating paths once lost,
Guiding us, no matter the cost.

Above the mist, the sun ascends,
A promise kept that never ends.
Through shadows deep, it breaks the night,
Transcendent light, a gift from sight.

With every ray, the heart ignites,
Unraveling dreams with pure delights.
In silent praise, the world will spin,
Where hope and love forever begin.

Embrace the warmth; let it inspire,
For in its glow, we lift our choir.
Together we'll touch the sky,
In transcendent moments, none shall vie.

So dance among the floating beams,
Awake your spirit, chase your dreams.
In light's embrace, we find our truth,
A radiant bond that knows no sleuth.

Chasing Fireflies in the Ether

Amidst the dusk, the magic glows,
Tiny sparks in soft repose.
We wander trails of twilight dreams,
Where laughter dances, joy redeems.

Through whispers faint, the night reveals,
Illuminated paths that feel.
We reach for stars, unbound, alive,
In this realm, our spirits thrive.

With every flicker, hearts align,
A fairy tale woven divine.
As fireflies weave their charming art,
They light the way, igniting heart.

In joyful chase, we cast away,
The weight of life, the pull of day.
With open hands, we'll catch the glow,
In fleeting moments, love will grow.

So hold the light, embrace the night,
With every spark that feels so right.
Together, through this dreamy air,
Chasing fireflies, free of care.

Resonance of a Dusk's Embrace

As shadows fall, the day concedes,
Embraced by hues, the world then breathes.
A gentle sigh, the night takes hold,
In warmth of dusk, our hearts unfold.

Subtle whispers in the breeze,
Carrying secrets through the trees.
In twilight's grace, we seek the peace,
Resonance found, our souls release.

Beneath the stars, we gather near,
In every laugh, in every tear.
The silent bonds that dusk bestows,
In tender light, our magic flows.

With every heartbeat, time stands still,
The world beyond fades, yet we thrill.
In this embrace, the night, our muse,
Resonance strong, we never lose.

So take my hand, let's journey forth,
In dusk's embrace, we find our worth.
Together in this twilight scene,
Resonance blessed, forever keen.

Celestial Chords in the Evening

As daylight wanes, a symphony starts,
Notes of twilight play on hearts.
In harmony, the stars align,
Celestial chords, a love divine.

With gentle plucks, the night unfolds,
A serenade that never grows old.
The moonlit sky, a canvas wide,
Where dreams take flight, and hope resides.

In every sound, a tale emerges,
As cosmic echoes, our spirit surges.
Through silver threads of starry lace,
We dance together, a timeless grace.

As shadows creep, the music swells,
In whispered notes, our longing dwells.
With every chord, our souls entwine,
In evening's glow, we find our shine.

So let us play beneath this dome,
In celestial songs, we find our home.
Together lost in twilight's cheer,
Celestial chords, forever near.

Whispering Clouds

In the sky, soft whispers roam,
Dancing light on azure dome.
Cotton dreams in gentle sway,
Lifting hearts, they drift away.

Veils of white in sunlight's grasp,
Hold the secrets, soft and vast.
Each breath escapes, a silent prayer,
Lost in wonder, floating air.

Storms may come to shake their form,
Yet they waltz, a peaceful norm.
In their dance, the world takes pause,
Nature's art, without a cause.

As the twilight brings its hue,
Clouds embrace the night in blue.
Stars peek through, a twinkling cheer,
A whispered promise, always near.

So let us gaze and drift along,
In clouded dreams, we all belong.
With every breath, we find our way,
In whispered clouds, we'll softly stay.

The Color of Solitude

A quiet room, shadows play,
Hints of blue bring thoughts to stay.
Softly wrapped in velvet night,
Lonely whispers dim the light.

The color speaks of silent fears,
Treasured hopes, and unseen tears.
Each wall holds a memory dear,
In solitude, they all draw near.

Outside, the world spins fast and bright,
While I linger, seeking light.
With every brush of fading sun,
A canvas waits for life's next run.

Yet in this space, I find my peace,
As fragile thoughts slowly release.
In shades of blue, my heart takes flight,
The color of solitude feels right.

Though time may pass and shadows shift,
In solitude, I find my gift.
A moment carved in quiet grace,
Embracing stillness, my sacred space.

Celestial Reverie

Underneath the midnight sky,
Stars are scattered, dreams can fly.
Whispers of the cosmos blend,
In their glow, we find a friend.

Galaxies swirl, a dance divine,
Echoes of a distant sign.
Every twinkle tells a tale,
In cosmic seas, we set our sail.

Moonlight weaves a silver thread,
Connecting hearts, the paths we tread.
In this reverie, souls ignite,
Guided gently by starlight.

Wishes float on astral breeze,
Carried softly, as we please.
Each moment holds a universe,
In celestial thoughts, we'll immerse.

Let the stars be our refrain,
In celestial dreams, we remain.
Beyond the earth, our spirits soar,
In the cosmos, forevermore.

Fragments of Light

In the dawn, shards gently gleam,
Whispers dance, a waking dream.
Colors burst in vibrant hues,
Painting life with morning's muse.

Sunlight filters through the trees,
Catching moments, like the breeze.
Each fragment sparkles, tender grace,
A fleeting touch, a soft embrace.

As day unfolds, shadows retreat,
Promises wrapped in warmth, we meet.
Fragments of laughter fill the air,
Joy cascades, a love to share.

In the evening, hues will fade,
Glowing softly, memories made.
Fragments linger, time stands still,
In every heart, a sacred thrill.

So let us gather, piece by piece,
In fragments of light, find our peace.
Together, we will light the night,
In every heart, a spark ignites.

The Heartbeat of the Cosmos

In the silence of the night,
Echos whisper through the dark.
Galaxies dance, a wondrous sight,
Each star a glowing spark.

Nebulas swirl in vibrant hues,
Painting dreams across the skies.
Time itself gently enthused,
Where every heartbeat never dies.

Orbiting worlds in perfect grace,
Waves of energy entwine.
A cosmic rhythm we embrace,
In this tapestry divine.

Awakening created light,
From depths of endless space.
A symphony of cosmic might,
In stillness, we find our place.

The rhythm of existence sings,
A cosmic lullaby's embrace.
In the heart, the universe clings,
Eternally, we hold its trace.

Hints of Golden Light

Morning dew on petals bright,
Catches whispers of the dawn.
The world awakens, soft and light,
As the night begins to yawn.

Golden rays through branches peek,
Painting shadows on the ground.
Every moment feels unique,
In nature's hymn, we're all bound.

Birds take flight on warming air,
Chasing dreams in sunlit skies.
Hints of gold are everywhere,
In the dance of life, it lies.

Time moves gently, nothing rushed,
Savoring each precious day.
In this glow, our spirits flushed,
Every worry fades away.

Within the light, our hearts ignite,
In the beauty all around.
Hints of golden pure delight,
In this magic, we're unbound.

The Magic Between Stars

Whispers travel through the void,
Carrying wishes, hopes, and dreams.
Between the stars, we feel joy,
In the light, reality beams.

Invisible threads intertwine,
Uniting souls from far and near.
In the cosmos, we align,
A bond that casts away fear.

Every twinkle tells a tale,
Of love and loss, joy and pain.
In the silence, we set sail,
On starlit paths, we remain.

Cosmic dust, a sacred stream,
Filling space with brilliant light.
In the night, we dare to dream,
Finding solace in the sight.

The magic flows like gentle air,
In the vastness, we belong.
Between the stars, we lay bare,
Eternal echoes of our song.

Serene Horizons

Across the fields of golden grain,
Gentle breezes softly sigh.
Mountains rise, a proud domain,
Underneath the endless sky.

Waves of blue kiss sandy shores,
Nature's rhythm poised and free.
In the stillness, beauty soars,
Inviting us to simply be.

Morning mist on tranquil lakes,
Mirroring the world above.
Each reflection gently wakes,
With whispers of unspoken love.

Clouds drift slowly, dreams take flight,
Colors blend as day turns night.
In the twilight, pure delight,
Serene horizons set our sight.

Under stars, our worries fade,
Embracing peace, we find our way.
In nature's arms, we're unafraid,
On serene horizons, we stay.

An Ode to the Celestial Canopy

Above us stretches vast and wide,
A tapestry where dreams reside.
Stars like jewels in dark embrace,
Whisper secrets in endless space.

Clouds drift softly, shadows play,
Moonlight bathes the night's ballet.
Galaxies spin with gentle grace,
An ode to night in this sacred place.

In the silence, a symphony sings,
Of ancient tales and timeless things.
Constellations guide the lost,
Reminding all of beauty's cost.

The universe, a canvas grand,
Painted by a cosmic hand.
Wonders waiting to be found,
In the silence, beauty abound.

So lift your gaze to skies above,
And feel the pulse of endless love.
In every twinkle, a connection lies,
An ode to the celestial skies.

The Dance of Light and Shadow

In the dawn, the light awakes,
Casting patterns as it shakes.
Shadows stretch and softly fade,
In this radiant, fleeting parade.

Noon brings forth a vibrant flare,
Dancing brightly, a golden sphere.
Shadows cool in corners lie,
Whispers of the sun's goodbye.

As dusk approaches, hues ignite,
Painting the world with soft twilight.
The dance of light begins to slow,
While shadows drape the earth below.

Nightfall wraps in velvet cloak,
Stars emerge, the silence spoke.
A paradox of dark and bright,
In this wondrous dance of light.

So watch the play with open heart,
Embrace the beauty of each part.
Light and shadow, forever entwined,
In every moment, harmony defined.

Starlit Serenades

In the hush of evening's breath,
Stars appear, defying death.
Softly twinkling, a lullaby,
A serenade from the sky.

They weave tales of love and fate,
Guiding souls who linger late.
In the dark, a promise shines,
Whispers echo through the pines.

Beneath the moon's silvery gaze,
Hearts find peace in gentle ways.
Each star a note in cosmic song,
In harmony, we all belong.

With every glimmer, dreams take flight,
A symphony of pure delight.
What sorrows fade beneath their light,
As starlit serenades ignite.

So linger here, beneath the glow,
Let the melodies softly flow.
In the night, let your spirit soar,
To starlit serenades forevermore.

Ethereal Brushstrokes at Twilight

As daylight wanes, the colors blend,
Ethereal brushstrokes that transcend.
Peach and lavender take the stage,
Nature's canvas, a vibrant page.

Whispers of night begin to creep,
Painting shadows where secrets sleep.
The horizon blushes, soft and bright,
A fleeting glimpse of day's last light.

Clouds stir gently, brushed with gold,
Stories of the day unfold.
In twilight's glow, the world transforms,
In this magic, wonder warms.

Stars awaken, join the show,
In this theater of firefly glow.
Each moment captured, fleeting grace,
In ethereal hues, we find our place.

So pause awhile, breathe in the view,
Let the spirit feel anew.
Ethereal brushstrokes grace the skies,
In twilight's embrace where beauty lies.

Glimmering Realities

In shadows deep where dreams converge,
Awakening souls begin to surge.
A flicker shines, hope takes its flight,
Glimmering truths emerge in light.

Whispers soft of what's to be,
Painting futures vivid and free.
Stars align in the night's embrace,
Glimmering paths, a wondrous chase.

Through storms and trials we find our way,
Guided by light, we seize the day.
Every heartbeat a chance to shine,
Glimmering realities, yours and mine.

In every glance, connections spark,
A tapestry woven, bright in the dark.
With every step on this sacred ground,
Glimmering dreams, together we're bound.

So let us dance in this radiant glow,
With open hearts, let our spirits flow.
In glimmering realities, we shall see,
The beauty that lies in you and me.

Enigma of the Heavens

Beneath the vault of starlit skies,
Questions linger, subtle sighs.
What secrets hold the cosmic dawn?
Enigma whispers, beauty drawn.

Constellations twinkle, tales unfold,
Stories of love, of courage bold.
In every shadow, mysteries play,
Enigma of heavens, night and day.

Celestial dance, graceful and grand,
Time like sand slips through our hand.
Yet in the chaos, patterns weave,
Enigma invites us to believe.

Through endless void, we search for signs,
In stardust trails, our fate aligns.
As comets blaze through mystic skies,
Enigma sparks our dreams to rise.

So gaze above where wonders gleam,
In silence, we hear the cosmos' dream.
With each heartbeat, we're lucky to know,
Enigma of the heavens, eternally flow.

The Mystique of Dusk

As daylight fades, the shadows creep,
Draped in whispers, the world is deep.
Colors collide as day turns to night,
The mystique of dusk, a wondrous sight.

Crickets sing as soft winds call,
A gentle hush blankets all.
Mysteries linger in the twilight hue,
With the mystique of dusk come dreams anew.

Each fading ray, a story told,
Of secrets wrapped in shades of gold.
The world in calm, a soft caress,
The mystique of dusk, a sweet finesse.

Beneath the stars, we find our peace,
In the stillness, worries cease.
With open hearts, the night unfolds,
The mystique of dusk, a tale retold.

So cherish moments as night takes flight,
In the embrace of gentle night.
For in the dusk, we live and feel,
The mystique of dusk, forever real.

Radiant Echoes

In every word, a story flows,
A sound that dances, softly glows.
As laughter rings, the heart ignites,
Radiant echoes, pure delights.

Memories whispered on the breeze,
Timeless songs among the trees.
Every moment, cherished and bright,
Radiant echoes in shared light.

Through valleys deep and mountains high,
Resonating truths that never die.
In harmony, our spirits blend,
Radiant echoes, love won't end.

The universe speaks in vibrant tones,
Connecting hearts, the love it sows.
Together we rise, hand in hand,
Radiant echoes across the land.

So let the echoes linger long,
In every heartbeat, a sacred song.
In unity, we shall forever thrive,
Radiant echoes, keeping dreams alive.

Phantoms of Light

In shadows dance the fleeting beams,
A whisper woven through the seams.
They shimmer softly, hearts take flight,
These glowing forms, the phantoms of light.

Through twilight's veil, their figures glide,
In mystery's arms, they softly bide.
A tapestry of dreams takes shape,
In darkness vast, they softly drape.

They flicker where the silence dwells,
In echoes sweet, their story swells.
With every pulse, they gently weave,
A world unseen, bids us believe.

A silent touch, a fleeting kiss,
In gentle hues, they bring us bliss.
The night is bright with tales untold,
As phantoms dance, our hearts behold.

So linger here beneath the stars,
In whispered light, erase our scars.
For in this realm, we find our sight,
With every ghost, a spark ignites.

The Spectrum of Serenity

Beneath the sky, where colors blend,
A calmness lingers, dreams descend.
In hues of peace, the world awakes,
The spectrum bright, our spirit makes.

A gentle breeze, the colors sway,
With every shade, they softly play.
In tranquil moments, hearts align,
The spectrum speaks, a love divine.

From turquoise depths to golden rays,
In each soft note, the spirit stays.
A harmony in every hue,
The spectrum sings, its song so true.

In violet dusk, the stars come forth,
A canvas bright, reflecting worth.
With every brush, we paint our dreams,
In shades of peace, life softly gleams.

So breathe the colors, let them in,
With every wave, our souls begin.
In calm embrace, we find our way,
In the spectrum's heart, forever stay.

Ethereal Blossoms

A garden blooms in twilight's glow,
With petals soft, that ebb and flow.
Each blossom spins a tale of grace,
In gentle whispers, time's embrace.

They sway like dreams on morning's breath,
With echoes sweet of life and death.
In every hue, a hope ignites,
The ethereal blooms, our spirits light.

Through silver mist, their fragrance weaves,
A tapestry of hopes and leaves.
In nature's arms, our dreams take flight,
With every bloom, a soft delight.

From twilight's kiss to dawn's own hand,
These blossoms speak across the land.
In gardens pure, where miracles dwell,
Ethereal whispers cast their spell.

So wander here, and lose your way,
In every petal, let hearts sway.
For in this space, our souls shall thrive,
With ethereal flowers, we come alive.

Rays of Unseen Fantasies

In twilight's hush, the magic breathes,
With whispers soft, the heart believes.
A ray of dreams, a flicker's grace,
Unseen fantasies find their place.

They shimmer bright in hidden nooks,
In every glance, in storybooks.
The shadows play, the light will dance,
In realms of hope, we find our chance.

A gleam of truth in midnight's grasp,
In secret smiles, the visions clasp.
Through veils of night, the wonders hide,
Rays of fantasies, in hearts abide.

With every breath, the dreamers soar,
In endless light, they seek to explore.
The unseen realms hold treasures grand,
With rays that weave, our hearts expand.

So chase the light, embrace the night,
In every dream, there lies a sight.
For in the dark, the magic gleams,
With unseen rays, we chase our dreams.

Colorful Altitudes

Soaring high with wings of dye,
Painted skies where eagles fly,
Mountains draped in hues so bold,
Whispers of the tales they've told.

Valleys shimmer, filled with cheer,
Rainbow arching, bright and clear,
Each step on the vibrant ground,
Nature's palette, beauty found.

Clouds like cotton, soft and light,
Dancing with the dawn's first sight,
Colors blend in perfect peace,
In this place, the heart finds ease.

Sunset bursts in fiery blaze,
Fading light through evening haze,
Stars begin their nightly show,
In these heights, the spirits glow.

Dreams take flight on painted wings,
In this realm, the joy it brings,
Colorful altitudes inspire,
Filling souls with pure desire.

Shroud of Light

Veil of dawn, so soft and bright,
Cascading down, a warm invite,
Gentle rays, like whispers, play,
Wrapping earth to greet the day.

Morning breaks, the shadows flee,
In the glow, we feel so free,
Sunlit paths where dreams align,
Every step, a new design.

Through the mist, the sun ascends,
Illuminating, it transcends,
Promises of warmth and grace,
In this shroud, all fears erase.

Golden beams on leaves aglow,
Telling stories, soft and slow,
Every corner kissed with light,
Transforming dark into delight.

In twilight's hue, the day concludes,
Silhouettes in soft imbues,
Wrapped in love and gentle care,
This shroud of light, forever rare.

Glistening Second Wind

Whispers ride on autumn's breeze,
Carrying tales through the trees,
Rustling leaves, a vibrant show,
Energized, the spirit flows.

In the hush of golden hour,
Life ignites with newfound power,
Every heartbeat, strong and clear,
In this moment, feel no fear.

Rays of sun through branches peek,
Nature's pulse is strong, not weak,
Breath of life, like rivers twist,
In this dance, we must persist.

Moments glisten, spark like fire,
Fueling dreams, igniting desire,
With each step, we find our goal,
Glistening within the soul.

As the night begins to fall,
Hearts are lifted, standing tall,
In this twilight, courage blend,
Embrace the glistening second wind.

The Lure of Distant Suns

Wanderlust calls from afar,
Guided by a distant star,
Echoes of the unseen land,
Awakening the heart to stand.

Horizons stretch beyond the view,
Painting dreams in colors new,
Each horizon, a tale unfolds,
In the glow, the future holds.

Secrets lie in cosmic beams,
Tales carved from forgotten dreams,
Adventure beckons in the night,
With every spark, we take flight.

Through the void, the journey begins,
Chasing down those luminous sins,
The universe whispers low,
In its vastness, we must go.

As we chase that radiant flare,
Feel the thrill of the open air,
For in the lure of distant suns,
Life's true journey has begun.

Horizon's Heartbeat

In the twilight's glow, warmth resides,
A whisper of dreams where hope abides.
Colors clash in a soft embrace,
Time flows gently, at nature's pace.

Eyes aglow with the evening light,
Boundless skies prepare for night.
The sun dips low, a golden shore,
Awakening hearts to seek for more.

Breezes carry tales from afar,
Under the watch of a rising star.
Each heartbeat echoes, a story told,
Of journeys begun, of spirits bold.

The horizon sings in hues of red,
As day retreats, where shadows tread.
Footsteps linger on paths unseen,
Carrying hopes where dreams have been.

Rich horizons wait for those who dare,
To chase the moments floating in the air.
With an open heart and eyes so bright,
We will find our way through the night.

Celestial Tapestry

Stitching the stars with threads of light,
Weaving stories in the heart of night.
Each glimmer dances, vibrant and free,
A cosmic dance for you and me.

Galaxies spin in their endless play,
Drawing us closer, come what may.
The moonlight shimmers like silver lace,
Enveloping us in a wide embrace.

Constellations whisper dreams on high,
As we gaze up at the sprawling sky.
Fingers trace lines of ancient lore,
Binding the past to the present once more.

Shooting stars clad in wishes bright,
Illuminate paths through the velvety night.
In this vast realm, we seek and find,
The secrets of souls intertwined.

A tapestry woven of dreams and fate,
Each thread a heartbeat, a love innate.
In the silence, our spirits soar,
Connected forever, forevermore.

Night's Gentle Caress

The moon whispers softly to the trees,
As shadows dance in the gentle breeze.
Crickets serenade the starry sky,
While dreams take flight, our spirits high.

Veils of night wrap us in peace,
Offering solace, a sweet release.
Each twinkling star a lover's sign,
Promising moments, forever entwined.

The world slows down with a hush so sweet,
As hearts remember their rhythmic beat.
Soft are the secrets that night will share,
In the tender glow of twilight's glare.

Embrace the shadows, let worries fade,
In this sacred space, memories are made.
As night unfolds its gentle embrace,
We find our dreams in that timeless space.

In the stillness, we breathe and sigh,
As the stars blink softly, a lullaby.
Held by night in its warm remain,
We dance through dreams, unspoken, untamed.

Beyond the Ether

In realms where light and shadow blend,
Dreams take flight, unbound, transcend.
Thoughts like whispers, drifting near,
Beyond the ether, calling clear.

Through veils of mist, we wander free,
Seeking depths of what might be.
Each heartbeat pulses with vibrant grace,
As we embrace the infinite space.

Lost to time, yet woven tight,
In the fabric of the endless night.
Journeys surge through stars aglow,
Unveiling truths that we long to know.

With open hearts and minds awake,
We venture forth, no fear to break.
Beyond the ether, magic swirls,
As wonder ignites in fantastical whirls.

So let us tread on this sacred ground,
Where echoes of the universe resound.
Hand in hand, we'll take flight,
Into the cosmos, embracing the light.

Dichotomy of Light and Twilight

In the dawn's embrace, shadows fade away,
Colors dance bright, heralding the day.
Yet twilight whispers of secrets untold,
A gentle reminder of stories of old.

Day clings to dreams, in sunlight it gleams,
While twilight unfurls its enigmatic schemes.
Contrasting the glow of the sun's warm rays,
In the twilight's hush, the night softly plays.

With each fleeting moment, the sky transforms,
A canvas of beauty, where creation performs.
Light and dark twine in a tender embrace,
A dichotomy woven in celestial space.

Stars blink awake as the sun bids farewell,
In twilight's soft arms, all mysteries dwell.
Yet hope lingers on in the evening's soft light,
As dreams take their flight in the fall of the night.

In the heart of the dusk, where shadows must tread,
Life dances between what is living and dead.
Each moment a choice, to cherish or fight,
In the silent embrace of the twilight's soft bite.

Chasing the Sun's Last Breath

As daylight fades, horizons ignite,
Chasing the sun as it whispers goodnight.
Rays of gold shimmer on waves of the sea,
A fleeting moment, forever to be.

With fingers outstretched, we grasp at the light,
Each heartbeat echoes the call of the night.
In the fading warmth, we linger and pause,
With dreams like the clouds, in the twilight, we cause.

The sun dips low, casting shadows anew,
Painting the world in a soft, gentle hue.
With every breath taken in twilight's sweet air,
We chase after time, lost in dreams we declare.

A tapestry woven with dusk's silent thread,
As stars pierce the canvas, fearlessly spread.
The sun takes its bow, the curtain descends,
In the embrace of twilight, time gently bends.

Forever we chase the sun's last sweet breath,
In shadows that linger, we'll dance until death.
With hearts full of wishes, we rise and we fall,
In the glow of the dusk, forever enthralled.

Mysteries in the Celestial Gaze

Beneath a vast sky, where wonders reside,
Stars sing their secrets, no need to confide.
Galaxies swirl in a delicate dance,
Mysteries linger, inviting a chance.

The moon softly glows, a lantern in dark,
Leading the way with its gentle spark.
Constellations whisper their ancient lore,
In the quiet of night, we seek to explore.

Eyes turned upwards, in awe we remain,
In the silence of night, our thoughts intertwine.
Celestial bodies in endless display,
Hold truths of the universe, hidden away.

A tapestry woven from dreams and from stars,
The cosmos is vast, yet it feels like ours.
Each twinkle a story, each shadow a sign,
In the realm of the night, our spirits align.

In the dance of the cosmos, we find our place,
With hearts full of wonder, we glide through the space.
The mysteries linger, inviting our gaze,
In the silence of night, our souls set ablaze.

Celestial Whispers

In the hush of the night, when all is at rest,
The universe speaks, a soft, soothing quest.
Whispers of starlight, secrets unfold,
Echoes of ages in stories retold.

A tapestry woven with silver and blue,
The moon sheds its glow, revealing the true.
Celestial voices ignite in the air,
In the stillness, we listen, a moment to share.

Comets that streak like whispers in flight,
Painting the sky with a touch of pure light.
Each journey a heartbeat in the vastness we see,
An invitation whispered, forever to be.

Galaxies spin in a dance of delight,
Where shadows and wonders merge into night.
Celestial murmurs, fleeting yet clear,
In the stillness of time, we relish the near.

As we gaze up in wonder, hearts open wide,
The universe whispers, we follow the tide.
For in every starlight, in every soft sigh,
Are the sacred connections that reach through the sky.

Glowing Dreams in the Firmament

Stars shimmer bright in endless night,
Whispers of hopes take elegant flight.
Galaxies dance in a silent grace,
Painting our dreams in this vast space.

Moonbeams gently caress the ground,
In the quiet, peace is found.
Voices of night softly sing,
Wrapped in warmth that starlight brings.

With every breath, the cosmos sighs,
Cradling wishes beneath the skies.
Time drifts slowly as shadows blend,
In the stillness, dreams transcend.

Twinkling thoughts converse in sleep,
In the firmament, secrets we keep.
Every heartbeat, a distant star,
Guiding us home from afar.

Awake in wonder, the dawn appears,
Painting the night with golden tears.
In these glowing dreams, we find our way,
Awakening hope with each new day.

Illuminated Echoes of Dawn

Daylight breaks with a gentle touch,
Whispers in colors, they mean so much.
Golden rays weave through the trees,
Dancing softly in the morning breeze.

Each shadow fades, the night takes flight,
Illuminated dreams greet the light.
Moments captured in vibrant hues,
Echoes of laughter as dawn renews.

Songs of the birds fill the air,
Nature awakens with tender care.
Raindrops glisten on petals bright,
In this beautiful morning light.

With every breath, we start anew,
Chasing horizons in shades of blue.
Hope's reflection on glistening streams,
Guiding our hearts as we follow dreams.

The world blossoms, alive and free,
Illuminated echoes calling to me.
A symphony formed through whispers sweet,
In the dawn's embrace, our spirits meet.

Twilight's Brush on Silent Waters

Evening falls with a painter's grace,
Brush strokes of purple illuminate space.
Ripples shimmer in soft, muted light,
As the day bows down to the approaching night.

Clouds gather round in a misty hue,
Every whisper of breezes feels new.
Reflections dance on the tranquil bay,
Where dreams and twilight gently sway.

Mountains watch as shadows extend,
Nature's canvas seems to blend.
Stars peek through as the sun retreats,
In this serene world, our hearts find beats.

The sky ignites in a fiery blaze,
Marking the close of vibrant days.
Under the moon, we find our peace,
In twilight's embrace, all worries cease.

Silent waters, secrets unfold,
Whispers of stories yet to be told.
Eclipsed by night, new dreams arise,
Painted beneath the velvet skies.

Celestial Reflections in Stillness

In the silence, the stars convene,
Mirroring dreams in the night's serene.
Each gleam a thought, a wish so clear,
Celestial whispers that all can hear.

Moonlit waters hold secrets deep,
Guarding the visions of those who sleep.
Ripples of light on the mirrored surface,
In this stillness, we find our purpose.

Time stands still, the universe sings,
In the embrace of cosmic wings.
As constellations weave through the night,
Magnolia's scent carries pure delight.

Guardians of dreams in the endless sky,
Echo of stardust as they float by.
Reflections dance with a mystical grace,
Painting the canvas of our space.

In stillness, we find the pieces of gold,
Celestial stories in silence unfold.
With each heartbeat, a spark ignites,
Awake in wonder, chasing the lights.

Tranquil Luminescence

In whispers soft the night unfolds,
A dance of light, in shadows bold.
Stars flicker like dreams that weave,
A tapestry of peace, believe.

Moonlit paths that gently guide,
Through tranquil lands where secrets hide.
Each glow a promise, sweetly spun,
In heart's embrace, the world is one.

Lakes reflect the night's caress,
Ripples whispering, never less.
A symphony of night's embrace,
Capturing time in silent grace.

Breezes carry tales untold,
Of ancient nights and hearts of gold.
In tranquil luminescence bright,
We find our dreams take flight tonight.

Celestial Blessings

From bows of heavens bright and wide,
Fall blessings like the stars abide.
A cosmic dance, a graceful leap,
In quiet moments, secrets keep.

Galaxies twirl, a radiant spin,
Whispers echo where love begins.
Comets trace our paths anew,
With every glance, the skies are blue.

Planets hum their ancient tune,
Under the watchful eye of the moon.
In starlit realms, our spirits soar,
Celestial gifts forevermore.

The universe in harmony,
In silent awe, we cease to be.
Embraced by wonders, hearts arise,
In celestial blessings, we find the skies.

Nebula in Bloom

Colors burst where darkness grew,
Nebula blooms, a vibrant hue.
Stars are born in spirals bright,
Cradled close, they welcome light.

Within the depths, a story spun,
Of cosmic dust and battles won.
Each swirl a memory, wild and free,
Painting dreams in eternity.

Swathes of red, and hints of blue,
Echoes of love, forever true.
In infinite space, hope takes flight,
With every bloom, a new delight.

Wisps of gas, a gentle sigh,
Cradle the stars as they rise high.
Nebula whispers, "Life renews,"
Amidst the night, as beauty brews.

Sunlit Secrets

Morning breaks, soft and golden,
Unveiling tales, long forgotten.
Sun-kissed whispers, trees embrace,
In every beam, a sacred space.

Shadows dance upon the ground,
With secrets in their movements found.
Petals glisten, dew adorned,
In sunlight's glow, the heart is warmed.

Rays of hope in gentle streams,
Caress our souls, ignite our dreams.
Nature sings a melody,
Of sunlight's grace, in harmony.

In quiet corners, moments hold,
A canvas bright with stories told.
Sunlit secrets pause to share,
The beauty found in life's sweet care.

Zephyrs of Luminescence

Soft winds carry whispers low,
Under the moon's gentle glow.
Stars twinkle in the night's embrace,
Chasing shadows, leaving trace.

Dreams are woven through the air,
Flowing like silk, delicate and rare.
With each breath, a new tale spins,
As the dawn of waking begins.

In the hush where silence swells,
Mysteries hide, untold spells.
Nature sighs in serene delight,
Kissing the edges of the night.

Fleeting moments, lost yet found,
Drifting lightly, tethered to ground.
Illuminated by love's embrace,
In the depths of endless space.

And as the luminescence fades,
Memories linger where hope pervades.
We dance with shadows, hand in hand,
In zephyrs of a dream-like land.

Elysian Horizons

Golden rays kiss the morning dew,
Awakening dreams, fresh and new.
Fields of blooms stretch far and wide,
Where endless joys and wonders hide.

Mountains rise, majestic and grand,
Whispers of secrets etched in sand.
Each horizon a canvas bright,
Painting pathways through the light.

With every step, a heartbeat's song,
A melody where we belong.
Together we stroll through this land,
Writing stories, hand in hand.

The sun dips low, a fiery glow,
Embracing us, as night winds blow.
Stars emerge, shy yet bold,
Each one a tale, waiting to be told.

In this realm of endless skies,
We find our truths, cast off the lies.
Elysian dreams shall weave and play,
Guiding us along our way.

The Illumination of Dreams

In the heart of night's embrace,
Dreams emerge, a tranquil space.
Visions drift like softest light,
Illuminating darkest night.

Ideas dance on the edges, free,
Casting shadows, wild and spree.
Hope flickers in the stillness' breath,
Bringing life, defying death.

Whispers echo, secrets told,
In dreams, the shy become bold.
Each dream a spark, a flame's delight,
Guiding souls through the night.

With every dawn, they softly fade,
Yet leave their mark, unafraid.
The heart remembers what the mind can't see,
In this realm, we find depree.

So we chase these phantoms bright,
With open hearts and souls alight.
For in the realm of dreams, we find,
Illumination of the heart and mind.

Whispering Luminosity

Gentle glimmers kiss the air,
Whispers of light, a secret flare.
A symphony of colors blend,
As day meets night, their paths wend.

Each flicker tells a hidden tale,
Of hopes that rise and fears that sail.
In shadows deep, a beacon glows,
Guiding hearts where love bestows.

The softest touch of golden rays,
Frames our lives in radiant ways.
In every heartbeat, soft and slow,
A world of wonder starts to grow.

As twilight settles, stars ignite,
Whispering secrets through the night.
In luminous dances, we entwine,
Finding solace, yours and mine.

In the silence, listen close,
To the whispers we cherish most.
For in the glow of shared delight,
We find our way, our guiding light.

A Canvas of Cosmic Light

In the vast embrace of night,
Stars twinkle, pure and bright.
Galaxies swirl, a dance so grand,
Whispers of the universe, hand in hand.

Brushstrokes of color, deep and wide,
Nebulas bloom, with pride they bide.
Celestial art, a cosmic view,
Every hue tells a tale anew.

Planets spin in silent grace,
Each one holds a secret place.
Comets dash through velvet skies,
In a flash, they mesmerize.

The moon unveils her silver sheen,
A beacon in the space unseen.
Timeless rhythms, the heavens play,
A symphony that stirs the day.

Every twinkling light a wish,
In the cosmos, dreams we fish.
A canvas vast, where hopes take flight,
Under the tapestry of night.

The Gossamer Veil of Night

A veil of dreams, so soft and light,
Wraps the world in gentle night.
Stars like whispers, secrets share,
Ethereal glow fills the air.

The quiet moon in silver crown,
Pours her light on sleepy towns.
Curled in shadows, soft and deep,
The world beneath begins to sleep.

Crickets sing their lullabies,
As the velvet darkness sighs.
In the stillness, magic weaves,
Through the branches, rustling leaves.

Fleeting dreams on softest air,
Glimmers dance without a care.
Wrapped in night's tender embrace,
We find comfort, a sacred space.

The gossamer veil draws near,
Whispers of night, sweet and clear.
In the hush, the heart takes flight,
Lost in the charm of the night.

Ethereal Glimmers Above

Ethereal glimmers, soft and bright,
Sparkle in the cloak of night.
Winking stars, in playful cheer,
Guide the dreams that linger near.

Where wonders unfold in cosmic sea,
Mysteries wait for you and me.
Twilight dances in colors rare,
Every moment, a breath of air.

Celestial wonders, bold and clear,
Paint the sky, our thoughts they steer.
Hidden tales in the stardust weave,
In their glow, we dare believe.

Through the darkness, adventure calls,
In the night, where starlight falls.
Ethereal glimmers, so divine,
Guide our souls, the stars align.

With every shimmer, a wish takes flight,
A beacon of hope in the endless night.
In the silence, magic thrives,
Under the glow, our spirit jives.

Harmony of the Stellar Dawn

As dawn breaks across the sky,
A symphony begins to fly.
Harmony in hues of gold,
A tale of light, quietly told.

Stars fade softly, bowing low,
As the sun begins to glow.
Eclipsing nights, the day does grace,
A dance of light in endless space.

In the blush of morning's kiss,
A universe awakens bliss.
Each beam of sunlight, warmth extends,
A day begins as night suspends.

Whispers of the cosmos blend,
In a harmony, soft and grand.
Galaxies twirl in morning's light,
Painting dreams as day takes flight.

The stellar dawn, a canvas bright,
Promising wonders, taking flight.
In the chorus of the day, we find,
The harmony that binds mankind.

Glories of a Fading Day

The sun dips low, in hues so bright,
Casting shadows, fading light.
Whispers of winds, soft and low,
Embrace the night, as sunsets glow.

Golden rays kiss the line of trees,
Painting skies with evening breeze.
Nature holds its breath and waits,
As daylight yields to night's warm gates.

Stars awaken, twinkling wide,
In the comfort of twilight's tide.
Moonbeams dance on shimmering streams,
Entwining dreams with soft, sweet themes.

Colors blend, both bold and shy,
Fading whispers of the sky.
The world wraps in twilight's embrace,
Finding peace in this sacred space.

Each day ends with a silent sigh,
As glories fade, yet do not die.
In heart's memory, they remain,
A palette brushed with joy and pain.

Celestial Firewater

In the night where starlight gleams,
Firewater flows, igniting dreams.
Ethereal sparks in liquid form,
Painting the night with magic warm.

Galaxies swirl in a cosmic dance,
Dipping time in a trance-like chance.
Mysterious hues of deep ocean blue,
Whispers of moments, old and new.

Unseen currents draw hearts near,
Flow with the pulse of what we fear.
Every droplet, a story spun,
Celestial magic when day is done.

Through the cosmos, the essence flows,
Filling souls as the night wind blows.
Drink deep of the light, let worries fade,
In this celestial firewater cascade.

Awake the stars with laughter's call,
In the embrace of night, we fall.
For in this silence, we find our way,
With celestial firewater, come what may.

The Magic of Waning Light

The sun retreats, the shadows sigh,
Waning light, a soft goodbye.
Golden glimmers on fields of green,
In the dusk, a tranquil scene.

Crickets sing their evening song,
Echoes of day that linger long.
The horizon blushes, deep and wide,
Inviting dreams from the other side.

With each breath of cooling air,
A sense of wonder, everywhere.
The magic stirs within our hearts,
As daylight fades and night departs.

Time slows down, a gentle pause,
Awakening in nature's laws.
Moments clasped in twilight's glow,
As secrets whisper, softly flow.

In this space where day meets night,
The magic dances in soft light.
Hold on tight to the fleeting day,
As it melts gently, fades away.

Betwixt Day and Night

In the hush where shadows blend,
Day and night begin to mend.
Colors merge, a soft bouquet,
Bathed in gold, then silver spray.

Glimmers wink from fading skies,
As twilight whispers, softly lies.
Moments linger in twilight's ring,
Hold your breath for the night to sing.

Dappled dreams mix with dusk's embrace,
Sprinkling hopes across time and space.
Each heartbeat merges with the breeze,
On scent of jasmine, hearts find ease.

A dance of shadows, flickering light,
Betwixt the day, the coming night.
In this twilight, magic sways,
In timid steps, where longing plays.

Through the portal of the skies,
In realms where dreams and starlight rise.
Cradle the moment, hold it tight,
For in between, lies infinite light.

Nightfall's Golden Breath

The sun dips low, the sky ignites,
With hues of gold and soft goodnights.
Stars awaken in the dusky light,
As day surrenders, yielding to night.

Shadows stretch on the silken ground,
In quiet whispers, peace is found.
The moon ascends with silver grace,
A gentle sigh in a tender space.

Crickets serenade the cooling air,
While fireflies dance without a care.
Each breath of dusk, a sweet embrace,
In night's caress, we find our place.

Clouds drift lazily, wrapped in dreams,
Soft lullabies on starlit beams.
With every heartbeat, time stands still,
As nightfall weaves its magic thrill.

In golden breath, the world transforms,
Wrapped in stillness, where love warms.
Each moment glows, forever bright,
In night's embrace, we take our flight.

The Symphony of Cosmic Glow

In velvet skies, the stars align,
A cosmic dance, a grand design.
Each note a twinkle, soft and bright,
Guiding our hearts through endless night.

Galaxies whirl in radiant hues,
Painting the canvas with vibrant views.
A symphony made of light and sound,
In every heartbeat, joy is found.

Nebulas bloom in colors rare,
Whispers of stardust fill the air.
In cosmic rhythms, we take our place,
A harmony of time and space.

Shooting stars make wishes fly,
In the silence, we dream and sigh.
With every glance, our spirits soar,
In the vastness, we yearn for more.

Beneath the cloak of night's embrace,
The universe holds a sacred space.
A symphony of cosmic light,
Enfolding us in pure delight.

Whispers of the Ethereal Heavens

Above the world, where dreams take flight,
Whispers linger in the moonlight.
Ethereal glimmers cascade down,
Painting our thoughts with their soft crown.

Celestial wonders call our name,
In secret echoes, they fan the flame.
Comets trail with shimmering grace,
Leaving behind a timeless trace.

In this realm of twilight's glow,
We share our secrets, few could know.
With every sigh, the stars reply,
A cosmic bond that will not die.

Luminous dreams weave through the night,
Illuminating hearts with their light.
In stillness found, we listen close,
To whispers where the heavens boast.

In ethereal realms, we float away,
On silver beams at the break of day.
Carried by hope, we touch the sky,
In whispered prayers, we learn to fly.

Colorful Horizons and Silent Wishes

At dawn's first light, horizons glow,
Brushed with colors, soft and slow.
Wishes carried on the morning breeze,
Whispered softly among the trees.

Each hue a promise, each shade a dream,
Painting the world with joy's sweet theme.
In every corner, hope ignites,
A canvas bright beneath the lights.

The sun ascends, warming the day,
Golden beams chase shadows away.
In the silence, hearts entwine,
Finding solace in the divine.

Beneath the arch of endless skies,
Silent wishes begin to rise.
Floating gently on a playful wind,
In colorful tapestries, they blend.

As night descends, colors fade,
But dreams remain, unafraid.
With every star, a wish is cast,
In vibrant hues, forever vast.

Wonders Beyond the Stratosphere

Stars whisper secrets, glowing and bright,
Galaxies dancing in the velvet night.
Planets in harmony, a cosmic embrace,
Mysteries linger in the endless space.

Comets like arrows through darkness do streak,
Carving a path, they shimmer and speak.
Nebulas swirl, a painter's delight,
Colors entwined, a breathtaking sight.

Amongst the silence, we yearn to explore,
Finding the wonders that lie at the core.
Infinite realms where wishes take flight,
Filling our hearts with celestial light.

Echoes of laughter from ages long past,
Visions unending, a spell that will last.
Beyond the horizon, the dreamers will soar,
To chase the adventures that wait to adore.

In the tapestry woven by fate and the stars,
We stitch our hopes, no matter how far.
Wonders await in the vast, chill expanse,
Each moment a chance for a cosmic romance.

Radiance of the Infinite Above

A canopy glimmers with light from afar,
Soft whispers of cosmos invite us to spar.
Constellations beckon, their stories unfold,
Each twinkle a promise, each flicker a gold.

Moonlight descends, casting shadows so light,
Guiding lost wanderers through the calm night.
Rays of the sun weave through clouds like a thread,
Kissed by the heavens, our spirits are fed.

Stars play the music of worlds yet unseen,
Harmonizing moments in vibrant sheen.
Planets align, creating rhythms divine,
In the grand orchestra, our hearts intertwine.

Time stands suspended, a dance in the void,
While galaxies swirl, we're blissfully awed.
Radiance shines brighter than any of gold,
Heartfelt connections in eternity's fold.

Through the darkness, the light finds its way,
Guiding the dreamers who wander and sway.
In the embrace of the infinite night,
We gather our wishes and hold them so tight.

The Infinity of Colored Dreams

In a realm of colors, where visions ignite,
Dreams stretch like rainbows, a stunning sight.
Petals of petals, the blossoms that bloom,
Each hue an emotion, dispelling the gloom.

Whispers of orange and soft shades of blue,
A symphony painted with every hue.
Golden horizons where daylight departs,
Cascading reflections through curious hearts.

In gardens of yearning, thoughts start to blend,
Each moment creates its own vibrant trend.
While night brushes softly with its cool embrace,
Colored dreams linger, time cannot erase.

A canvas of wonder, we splash on the screen,
Living the stories that color our scene.
With each sleeping promise and dream that we weave,
Infinity beckons, inviting to believe.

Through dreams we wander, our spirits take flight,
Chasing horizons that soften the night.
In the galaxy's arms, we're forever entwined,
Living the colors, a love undefined.

Fading Echoes of Daylight

As daylight retreats, the shadows arise,
Echoes of laughter fade into the skies.
Whispers of dusk sing a lullaby sweet,
Gentle reminders of moments we meet.

The sun bids farewell, painting the dark,
Starlight ignites, life's fragile spark.
Memories linger in twilight's embrace,
Reflections of dreams, like a soft lace.

Fading echoes, they dance on the breeze,
Carrying voices from the close of the trees.
A tapestry woven of silken threads,
In the hush of the night, all our concerns shed.

Through shadows we wander, the past ever near,
Hopes like the twilight slowly appear.
Fleeting as gossamer, time drifts away,
In the fading echoes, we cherish the day.

As night cloaks the world, we settle our minds,
In the stillness, a peace we shall find.
Fading echoes linger, like stars up above,
In the softness of dusk, we remember our love.

Heaven's Palette

Colors blend across the sky,
Painting dreams as clouds drift by.
Each hue whispers soft and sweet,
Where earth and heavens gently meet.

Golden rays embrace the dawn,
Awakening the world reborn.
With lavender and blush's sigh,
Nature sings, and angels fly.

Crimson blossoms bathe in light,
Guiding souls through day and night.
In twilight's grasp, a canvas spread,
Where whispered hopes and wishes tread.

Stars emerge, a velvet cloak,
In the silence, shadows spoke.
A symphony of faintest glows,
In heaven's palette, magic flows.

As night unfurls her jeweled hand,
We dance upon the stardust sand.
In every shade, our dreams align,
In this celestial design.

Enchanted Twilight

The sun dips low, a gentle tease,
As whispers sigh upon the breeze.
Soft twilight wraps the world in grace,
An enchanted, timeless space.

Shadows stretch, entwined with light,
Crafting secrets of the night.
In hues of purple, deep and rare,
Moments linger, still and fair.

The moon awakens, bright and bold,
Spinning tales that must be told.
Stars ignite in silver trails,
On whispered winds, where magic sails.

A hush descends, like velvet cloth,
As dreams unfurl, our hearts take oath.
In twilight's arms, we find our song,
An echo where we all belong.

With every breath, the night unfolds,
A treasure trove of dreams untold.
In enchanted twilight's glow,
Together, through the stars, we flow.

Vivid Realms Above

High above, where skies ignite,
Vivid dreams take off in flight.
Bold horizons stretch so wide,
In realms where wonders always hide.

Clouds like cotton, soft and bright,
Dancing gently, pure delight.
Sunsets burst with fiery hues,
In each brushstroke, life renews.

Galaxies twirl in cosmic dance,
Inviting souls to take a chance.
Amidst the stars, our spirits roam,
In vivid realms, we find our home.

Through astral gates, we journey forth,
Discovering the hidden worth.
In every shimmer, every glow,
Tales of love and hope bestow.

From dawn to dusk, the colors blend,
In vibrant tales that never end.
With every glance, the skies do call,
In vivid realms, we dance, we fall.

Celestial Sojourn

In twilight's arms, we start to soar,
A celestial sojourn, forevermore.
With stars as guides, our hearts take flight,
On pathways woven with purest light.

Through endless skies, we wander far,
Chasing dreams beneath each star.
In cosmic mists, we find our place,
Among the heavens, full of grace.

Galactic whispers softly call,
Inviting us to rise and fall.
The universe sings, a sweet refrain,
In every heartbeat, love's sweet chain.

Meteor trails mark paths of hope,
In the darkness, we learn to cope.
Each moment fleeting, yet so dear,
In celestial sojourn, we persevere.

As we traverse the starlit sea,
The cosmos unfolds its mystery.
In dreams alight, we find our way,
Forever seeking the break of day.

Dancing Colors in Twilight

Shadows stretch as daylight fades,
Painting skies in vibrant shades.
Crimson whispers gently rise,
In the quiet, color sighs.

Gentle breezes softly sway,
Carrying the night away.
Orange blooms, the last sun's kiss,
In this moment, feel the bliss.

Softly twinkle, stars appear,
Bringing night-time's magic near.
Lavender drapes the fading light,
Dancing colors, pure delight.

Golden hues begin to fade,
As the twilight serenade.
Each tone merges, smiles unfold,
In the beauty, hearts are bold.

From the blues to deepest grey,
Nature whispers, come and stay.
In the twilight's warm embrace,
Time stands still in this sweet space.

Celestial Whispers at Dusk

As the sun dips low, so bright,
Moonbeams kiss the edge of night.
Stars begin their gentle dance,
In this twilight, find romance.

Crickets sing in soft refrain,
Nature's lullaby, unchained.
In the dark, the world's aglow,
Whispers carry, moving slow.

Eyes closed tight, we catch a dream,
Floating on the silver beam.
Moments lost, yet held so dear,
In celestial whispers clear.

With every breath, the stillness grows,
A tapestry no one knows.
Painted skies in shades of blue,
Dusk unveils a world that's true.

Feel the magic, quiet night,
Hear the stars, their voices light.
Wrapped in velvet, time unwinds,
In these moments, peace we find.

The Luster of Evening Stars

Silken skies hold dreams in sight,
Evening stars begin their flight.
Sparkling luster, soft and clear,
Glimmers shine, the night is near.

Cascading light from far away,
Guides the heart, paves the way.
Constellations tell their tales,
In the silence, wonder sails.

With each twinkle, wishes soar,
While the universe gives more.
Galaxies whisper in the dark,
Awakening a hidden spark.

Infinite, the night unfolds,
Mysteries in silver molds.
Underneath this velvet dome,
Every heart can find its home.

Dreamers gaze and hands reach high,
Touching echoes of the sky.
In their glow, we find our way,
Stars will guide us, night and day.

Radiant Hues of the Horizon

Morning breaks with colors bold,
Radiant hues, a sight to behold.
Vanishing night, in shades of gold,
A symphony of warmth unfold.

Soft pastels in gentle flight,
Brush the canvas, pure delight.
Pink and orange kiss the seas,
Whispers dance upon the breeze.

Horizon stretches, infinite line,
Nature's palette, pure design.
As dawn awakens, spirits rise,
Wonders painted across the skies.

Each new day brings hope anew,
In the light, we find our view.
Colors merge, a sweet refrain,
Beauty lingers after rain.

From the dawn to daylight's end,
Nature bends, but will not mend.
Radiant hues remind us clear,
Life's a canvas, full of cheer.

Milton Keynes UK
Ingram Content Group UK Ltd.
UKHW010232111224
452348UK00011B/704